DYING
to meet
HIM

Marjorie E. Hopkins

DYING
to meet
HIM

Wit and Wisdom from
a Funeral Director's Wife

TATE PUBLISHING
AND ENTERPRISES, LLC

This book is designed to provide accurate and authoritative information with regard to the subject matter covered. This information is given with the understanding that neither the author nor Tate Publishing, LLC is engaged in rendering legal, professional advice. Since the details of your situation are fact dependent, you should additionally seek the services of a competent professional.

The opinions expressed by the author are not necessarily those of Tate Publishing, LLC.

Published by Tate Publishing & Enterprises, LLC
127 E. Trade Center Terrace | Mustang, Oklahoma 73064 USA
1.888.361.9473 | www.tatepublishing.com

Tate Publishing is committed to excellence in the publishing industry. The company reflects the philosophy established by the founders, based on Psalm 68:11,
"The Lord gave the word and great was the company of those who published it."

Published in the United States of America

ISBN: 978-1-61346-489-2
1. Religion: Christian Life, Inspirational
2. Religion: Christian Life, Death, Grief, Bereavement
11.09.19

DEDICATION

This work is dedicated to DePauw University, my alma mater, to fulfill a promise I made to Louis J. Fontaine, '52, who served DePauw in various capacities during his long career with the university. While director of admissions and financial aid in the late 1970s, he arranged for special financial assistance for me for my senior year and secured my promise that my first book would be dedicated to the university. Thank you, Mr. Fontaine: Here's to you and to DePauw!

ACKNOWLEDGMENTS

To my family, especially my Christian parents, now with God, and to my "beautiful feet" ministers, who brought the Word of God to me through my youthful years and who laid a solid biblical foundation for the building blocks of my life and walk with God. These ministers include, but are not limited to, Donald E. Christy, Fred Williams, Cletis Ellett, Leo Miller, Larry Branam, and Donald H. Christy—honorable men of God with beautiful feet! "…It is written, 'How beautiful are the feet of those who bring good news!'" (Romans 10:15, NIV)

TABLE OF CONTENTS

INTRODUCTION

…Death is the destiny of every man; the living should take this to heart.

Ecclesiastes 7:2 (NIV)

When I was young, I feared death, and I prayed constantly to God that I would have a better understanding of death so I would not be afraid of it but could even accept it in times of Christian persecution, if needed. I wanted to be able to say, like Paul, "For to me to live is Christ and to die is gain… I am torn between the two" (Philippians 1:20-23, NIV).

I think it's rather humorous that I felt God led me to marry a funeral director. It certainly wasn't the way I expected my prayers to be answered! Through this experience I came to believe that God

…Death is the destiny of every man; the living should take this to heart.
Ecclesiastes 7:2 (NIV)

11

uses humor sometimes to teach us. So you will find that most chapters of this book begin with a rather entertaining story from my funeral home days that ties in with a spiritual reflection upon the same subject. I believe God taught me much about death and, in consequence, life while I served as the wife of a funeral director. I learned much of this reflecting back on my time at the funeral home. I'd like to share what I learned with you because I believe, all across the world, God is calling all of His children out of a lukewarm relationship into a higher, deeper, and more purposeful relationship with Him. In this complicated and turbulent world, we all need more than a superficial relationship with our Maker and Lord—the days of complacency should be over for all of us, as all around us people are searching more than ever for that "something" they are missing. And in the midst of it all, Christian persecution is on the rise in other countries, but especially here at home in America, a nation that was created under God and on Christian principles and a place where Christians' faith and strengths have really not been tested.

In all of these circumstances, we need an *eternal* relationship with God—one that begins here

…Death is the destiny of every man; the living should take this to heart.
Ecclesiastes 7:2 (NIV)

and is culminated at our death—a relationship in which we are so in love and in awe of God that we are willing to both live and die for Him, a relationship in which we truly are *dying to meet Him* face-to-face.

—Marjorie E. Hopkins

...Death is the destiny of every man; the living should take this to heart.
Ecclesiastes 7:2 (NIV)

13

A Note to the Reader

On the following pages, you won't find a story that is woven throughout each chapter with a hero/heroine, a plot, and a nail-biting conflict and conclusion. You *will* find a series of short stories that can stand alone but yet have a common theme running throughout them—the theme of thinking *eternally* vs. thinking of the *here and now* of this world. This *is* a busy world, and most of us have hectic lives with little time to spare for luxuries like reading and deep thinking. I have kept that in mind and made this book a short, easy read—one that you might be able to complete in a morning or afternoon over a cup of coffee—but I hope and pray that the messages inside are eternal ones. I pray they are ones you will remember throughout your

...Death is the destiny of every man; the living should take this to heart.
Ecclesiastes 7:2 (NIV)

15

life so that the passage from this here-and-now life into the eternal life is an easy one and an anxiously anticipated one—so that you will truly be dying to meet Him!

...Death is the destiny of every man; the living should take this to heart.
Ecclesiastes 7:2 (NIV)

We'll Be the Last to Let You Down: A Funeral Director

> Humble yourselves, therefore, under God's mighty hand, that he may lift you up in due time. Cast all your anxiety on Him because He cares for you.
>
> 1 Peter 5:6-7 (NIV)

"Mom, what in the world should I do? Should I go?"

I had just been asked a question that was most unusual, and I'll wager it's a question not many people have been asked. I *could* possibly be the only one—*ever*. I was twenty-four years old, just out of college. I moved out of my lifelong home

…Death is the destiny of every man; the living should take this to heart.
Ecclesiastes 7:2 (NIV)

17

with my parents to a small town about eighteen miles away. I was hired as a writer for a radio station where, one day, I was introduced to Mark. His parents owned a local funeral home, and he and his dad were funeral directors. A date soon followed after Mark and I met. Then there were others. But one I distinctly remember. Mark and I had a date scheduled, actually one of our very first dates, and he called to cancel it because he had to go to a nearby airport to pick up a body that was being flown in from out of state. (This is something that happens occasionally at funeral homes when a person is on vacation or visiting out of town and dies unexpectedly. The body is then flown home, and it is the job of the funeral director to retrieve it from the airport.)

Mark explained the situation to me and said, "I'll have to cancel—unless you want to go with me?" I didn't know what to say. I didn't give him a definite yes or no at that moment. *What an interesting date that would be!* I thought. I said I would get back with him. I hung up and called my mom—I always went to my mom for good advice. We were very close.

...Death is the destiny of every man; the living should take this to heart.
Ecclesiastes 7:2 (NIV)

DYING to meet HIM

"Well," she said, "if you like him, you better get used to it." I did like Mark. I liked him a lot. I ended up going with him to pick up the body. It was the first of many times that I went with Mark to pick up bodies, to pick up death certificates, to deliver funeral flowers, to help at visitations and funerals. I became the wife of a funeral director.

Death. I was around it daily. It was something I had feared for years. Being a Christian, I knew I should not fear it because of my belief that Jesus had made a way for me—for humanity—to be able to live eternally with Him. I had prayed all of my life to not be afraid of death. So here I was, face-to-face with a fear that I had had all my life. I've always heard that you usually fear something that you are not familiar with. Well, I got to see at least the physical side of death, and I became very familiar with it. I came to understand it a little better. When you're surrounded by death, somehow you do become a little better acquainted with it, and I was around it *all* the time as the wife of a funeral director.

I didn't realize just how much I had learned about death (and in consequence, life) but now,

…Death is the destiny of every man; the living should take this to heart.
Ecclesiastes 7:2 (NIV)

19

as I reflect back, I can see that God was teaching me about death in many ways. My prayers of many years were being answered in the most unusual way.

Even though the funeral business was a very serious business and my in-laws were extremely conscientious about providing the best possible service to the families who entrusted their loved ones to them, we tried to make some lighter moments to the business—at least within the family. You just can't live day to day with the somber subject and all the grief you faced without a few moments of laughter and lightheartedness. I used to joke around and tell my friends that we'll be the last to let you down! At least we would be the last to let you down—literally—in a grave on this earth.

But God will never let us down. If we humble ourselves and do His will in our lives, and if we are in a relationship with Him, He will lift us up, even as we face death. If He is our God, He will be there.

"Yea, though I walk through the valley of the shadow of death, I will fear no evil: for thou art with me; thy rod and thy staff they comfort me" (Psalm 23:4, KJV). He won't let us down into a grave

...Death is the destiny of every man; the living should take this to heart.
Ecclesiastes 7:2 (NIV)

without raising us up. He will always be there for us in this life before death. We should have no fears—no fears in life or in death. He will be there. I just pray that we will be there for Him in world that is dying without Him. And it's also my prayer that if you aren't already just dying to meet God face-to-face, you soon will be.

Summary
"We'll Be the Last to Let You Down: A Funeral Director"

As the wife of a funeral director, God taught me a lot about a subject that I had feared most of my life: death. My first lesson was that if I have the relationship with God that He wants me to have, I should not fear anything, especially death. He will never leave us, and He won't let us down into a grave without raising us up to be with Him forever. If we know Him as our Savior in life, He will be our Savior in death. But we also need to be there for Him in a world that is searching for Him and dying without knowing Him.

...Death is the destiny of every man; the living should take this to heart.
Ecclesiastes 7:2 (NIV)

Questions

Is death something you think about? Why or why not?

_____

_____

_____

_____

Should we as Christians think about death? Why or why not?

_____

_____

_____

_____

_____

...Death is the destiny of every man; the living should take this to heart.
Ecclesiastes 7:2 (NIV)

Should we teach our children about death? Why or why not?

_____

_____

_____

_____

How imminent do you think your death is?

_____

_____

_____

Are you afraid to die? If so, why?

_____

_____

_____

_____

...Death is the destiny of every man; the living should take this to heart.
Ecclesiastes 7.2 (NIV)

From Life to Death:
A Mist, a Destiny

...What is your life? You are a mist that appears for a little while and then vanishes.

James 4:14 (NIV)

...Death is the destiny of every man; the living should take this to heart.

Ecclesiastes 7:2 (NIV)

I watched them come, day after day, week after week. Some came in the morning. Some came at night, but they came. They came in a constant movement. It was a parade of people from all walks of life. Some were poor. Some were rich. Some were uneducated. Some were edu-

...Death is the destiny of every man; the living should take this to heart.
Ecclesiastes 7:2 (NIV)

25

cated. Some were fat. Some were thin. Some were elderly. Some were babies. Some were well known. Others were not. The one thing that they all had in common was *death*.

It made me wonder if we ever really think about the fact that we're dying. Or are we too busy living to think about it? Do we realize that from the moment we are born, we are facing death? *It is the only certain thing in life.* I've heard there are only two certain things in life: taxes and death. But I know from experience that a person can die before he has to pay taxes. I've seen it happen. I know too that it's a sure bet you and I are going to die. Very few have avoided it. [Enoch was translated by God and never saw death (Genesis 5:23, 24). Elijah was carried by a whirlwind into heaven and bypassed death (2 Kings 2:11).]

I don't mean to sound dramatic. It's just a simple fact of life. From the moment we are born, we are facing death—both physical and spiritual. It isn't something that some of us have to face and others don't. It happens to young and old alike. It happens to the rich and poor, to smart and dumb.

...Death is the destiny of every man; the living should take this to heart.
Ecclesiastes 7:2 (NIV)

There is no distinction. There is no discrimination. It is a certainty. It is our destiny (Ecclesiastes 7:2).

And yet death is probably the one thing we prepare for the least. It is like the proverbial elephant in the room. It's there. It's huge. And everyone acts like it isn't there. Death. It is the one thing that nobody wants to talk about, let alone think about or discuss. And sadly, it's the thing most people don't spiritually prepare for.

We spend years preparing for life. We prepare for marriage. We prepare for a new home. We send our children to school. We save for their college. We give them music lessons. We make certain that they know about sports and all the so-called *important* things in life. We prepare them for jobs while we prepare for retirement. We oftentimes succeed in all these preparations acquiring all sorts of "stuff" to pass down to the next generation. Then we die, and our children spend time preparing their kids for life—before they die. But in the end, it's death that we all face, whether we're prepared to or not.

...Death is the destiny of every man; the living should take this to heart.
Ecclesiastes 7:2 (NIV)

The really sad thing is that we are, more often than not, shocked when death happens. I heard it almost daily. I've said similar things myself.

"He was so young!"

"She looked so good and seemed so happy."

"I can't believe he's gone!"

"I just saw her Monday, and she seemed fine."

Those are things often heard from those misty-eyed people who attended visitations and funerals.

Then there was the question most frequently asked: "Why?"

And then there's the saddest question of all: "Why did God do this?"

It's a question asked by those who haven't been spiritually prepared for death, spiritually prepared to accept it, face it, or experience it. We are given *no* promise as to when death will happen. We take for granted that death won't happen to us or to our families until—I'm not certain until what—old age? But I've seen how frequently it happens on a daily basis and how frequently it happens to those who are not expecting it to happen. Today could be my day, or it could be your day. We have no guarantees.

…Death is the destiny of every man; the living should take this to heart.
Ecclesiastes 7:2 (NIV)

I can assure you of one thing: it is something that God never intended to happen. We were not created to die but to live. It was our fault. It wasn't God's fault. In the garden called Eden, the Bible tells us that there was a tree of life and a tree of knowledge of good and evil. The only tree that Adam and Eve were not to eat from was the tree of knowledge of good and evil (Genesis 2:15-17). They had an intimate fellowship with God. As long as they obeyed, they lived and could eat from the tree of life and could walk and talk with God face-to-face.

But God gave them a choice, a free will. They were not made to be puppets. Satan tempted them with a lie (Genesis 3). They ate of the forbidden tree. Because of their sin, they were separated from God and His fellowship. Where once they walked and talked with God, they were now alone. They faced death, both physically and spiritually. Death was born into the human race that day. Death had come on the scene. There was now a separation between Almighty God and the creatures that He had created. Sin always separates us from Him. Because of sin, to this day, we all face the

...Death is the destiny of every man; the living should take this to heart.
Ecclesiastes 7:2 (NIV)

death sentence. "Therefore, just as sin entered the world through one man, and death through sin, and in this way death came to all men, because all sinned…"(Romans 5:12, NIV).

Our life here on earth is fleeting. We are truly but a mist that appears for a short while. And since it is but for a short time, doesn't it make sense to prepare for death and then live life to the fullest? I don't mean to constantly think about death. I'm talking about being secure in the fact that we have a future life—an eternal life that is much more significant than this physical one—a much, much longer one—one that has no end. And if we are truly prepared for death, it won't be something we will cringe from or something we will fear or not understand, but it will become that ultimate moment when we are to see our Maker face-to-face. It will be when we see the One who redeemed us by His Son, Jesus Christ, so our physical separation with Him is but fleeting—so it will be no longer than a vaporous mist.

I saw a bumper sticker the other day. It stated: "If You Are Living Like There Is No God—You Better Be Right!" I believe also that if we truly

…Death is the destiny of every man; the living should take this to heart.
Ecclesiastes 7:2 (NIV)

believe in God, we'd better be living like there is a God. I believe there are many who claim to be Christians today who truly don't live their faith or have a real, personal, and saving relationship with their Lord. There is superficiality to it—it's luke-warm. It is a relationship where God is not number one and where eternity is thought little of.

I heard a minister once declare that it would be better to go through this life as a Christian and at the end find that there was no heaven or hell than to go through this life as an atheist and find that there was an eternity and a heaven only for those who have Jesus as their Lord and Savior.

Personally, I have no doubt there is a God. I have no doubt that there is a place called heaven and there is a place called hell, that there is the utmost evil being called Satan, and that every person who walks the face of this earth will someday come face-to-face with their Holy Creator, God Almighty. I believe that we will spend eternity in one of two places, just as the Bible says. When I face that certainty called death, I want to be holding on to Jesus's hand to lead me to the other side. God has made that possible for all people; He has

...Death is the destiny of every man; the living should take this to heart.
Ecclesiastes 7:2 (NIV)

31

made it possible to face death without fear—and to face it with expectation and anticipation of something so wonderful we cannot even imagine it (1 Corinthians 2:9)!

There are many who face death alone. There are many who feel they are wandering through a mist in this life. There are many who are afraid of death. God calls us to renew a lost fellowship with Him through His Son, Jesus—a fellowship that will be made complete when we see Him face-to-face. It's a moment we should anticipate and long for. You may or may not believe all this, but there is one thing for certain: you are dying, and you better be thinking about it.

Summary
"From Life to Death: A Mist, A Destiny"

Death happens. It happens often. It happens daily. God doesn't want us to shirk from thinking about it. We prepare so diligently for life that is so fleeting but don't prepare for death that is so eternal and certain. We need to think eternally and begin to anticipate our face-to-face reunion with God Almighty, who loves us so much.

...Death is the destiny of every man; the living should take this to heart.
Ecclesiastes 7:2 (NIV)

Questions

Have you thought about how often and how quickly death happens?

_____

_____

_____

_____

_____

How do you prepare for this life? How do you prepare your children for this life?

_____

_____

_____

_____

_____

...Death is the destiny of every man; the living should take this to heart.
Ecclesiastes 7.2 (NIV)

Are you preparing for eternity? If so, how?

_____

_____

_____

_____

_____

Should we teach our children to prepare for death and eternity? If yes, how can we do this?

_____

_____

_____

_____

_____

…Death is the destiny of every man; the living should take this to heart.
Ecclesiastes 7:2 (NIV)

UNDER THE CASKET: LOOKING HEAVENWARD

The heavens declare the glory of God; the
skies proclaim the work of his hands.

Psalm 19:1 (NIV)

It happened during the cold of an Indiana win-
ter. Ice and snow covered the ground—always
an unpleasant thing when you are conducting a
funeral, especially at the graveside. Although I
wasn't a witness to this spectacle, I can still picture
it vividly in my mind.

The family and friends of the departed one
began arriving at the graveside, stepping around
cold stone markers, passing by an occasional dark-
gray, leafless tree silhouetted against a lighter gray

...Death is the destiny of every man; the living should take this to heart.
Ecclesiastes 7:2 (NIV)

sky. They made their way to the small tent to huddle into any warmth they could find. The cold wind—blowing, stinging—brought tears to the eyes of those whose eyes were still dry. The people finally gathered around in the small tent.

Fragile, brightly colored flowers in the tent seemed, I'm sure, totally out of place in the frosty stillness. There was the smell of cold, freshly dug dirt. There was crying, sniffing, whispering. The feeling of loneliness, the feeling of loss, was becoming more real to each one in attendance as they waited for the pallbearers who would bring the casket to its final resting place.

The young man in charge of the graveside ceremony opened the back of the funeral coach and grasped the end of the casket. The pallbearers behind him silently waited for their heavy burden. He started to pull the death-laden casket out like he would any other day, at any other funeral, expecting the same results that he had had on numerous previous occasions.

He pulled a little too hard, a little too quickly, while his feet were on ice, and lost his footing. His legs, straight and unbending, slid right under the

...Death is the destiny of every man; the living should take this to heart.
Ecclesiastes 7:2 (NIV)

funeral coach while his hands still clung to the casket. His body, lying perfectly straight under it, looked like a mechanic's body that had just slid under a car.

Actually, upon reflection, I don't think that it's too bad of a position for anyone to be in. He had a good view in that moment under the casket. It is a sight that I believe we all should see. If we were there on our back under the casket, it would be a place where we could see death in perspective. We could see it just above us, like the casket, something we have to face, and beyond it, eternity as we know it. For looking heavenward, we are looking at a form of eternity. In all of our so-called intelligence, we don't even know where the sky ends. We don't know where it begins. We don't know what's beyond. To us, it is infinite. It is eternal. We should often reflect on this spectacular form of eternity that we have right before us every day of our lives, reminding us of our *eternal* destiny. We all need to take a long hard look *heavenward*.

Our visual perimeter usually does not exceed our height. Of course, this is very practical for day-to-day living. We need to see where we have

…Death is the destiny of every man; the living should take this to heart.
Ecclesiastes 7.2 (NIV)

37

been, what we are passing over, and where we are going. Yet always looking down on the earth can be frightening, making us feel alone in our plight, and on the other hand, more often than not, it can also evoke a false sense of human pride. When we look around us, behind us, and below us, we see earth. We see the creation over which we were given dominion (Genesis 1:26). We grow accustomed to viewing nature with no great sense of awe. We see things that make us look powerful in proportion—we see the works of man's hands and tend to marvel over the construction of a building or the design of a new computer chip, architecture, or a spaceship.

I've come to love poetry over the years. One poem I recall studying while I was in college is called "Hawk Roosting" by Ted Hughes. In this poem, the hawk has such an elevated view of himself that he believes he revolves the earth. For it is only when he flies that the world appears to move.

Sometimes I think that is how humankind views humankind. We think we are all powerful, all knowing, all creating. I think many believe that it is we who *make the world go round* or we who

...Death is the destiny of every man; the living should take this to heart.
Ecclesiastes 7:2 (NIV)

revolve the earth. Yet the hawk needs only to look above to realize that he is not the one that rotates the earth—that something more omnipotent and omniscient exists. So do we. Look heavenward on a clear night and marvel at the stars that He "determines the number of" and "calls them each by name" (Psalm 147:4, NIV).

It is reported that Abraham Lincoln once said, "I can see how it might be possible for a man to look down upon the earth and be an atheist, but I cannot conceive how he could look up into the heavens and say there is no God."

If we would look heavenward more often, we would see the glory, the magnificence, the intricacy of the universe and know there is a God, that there is an eternity, and that He cares for us. If you can't see Him on the earth, you certainly will see Him in the heavens that "declare the glory of God" and the firmament that "proclaim the work of His hands" (Psalm 19:1, NIV). You will see Him in the infinite heavens where there is no beginning and no end known to man. How small and powerless we feel when we get a glimpse of eternity! How miniscule the works of man's hands become when we see the

...Death is the destiny of every man; the living should take this to heart.
Ecclesiastes 7.2 (NIV)

39

Marjorie E. Hopkins

heavens and contemplate. This contemplation can really put our lives in perspective and can cause us to think more *eternally*, more frequently, about our God and the purpose He has for us.

I remember a minister once telling his congregation that we would think he was absolutely crazy if he told us that the building we were in had no designer, no architect, and no one to construct it, that somehow the bricks just came together on top of a foundation that just happened to be. Somehow the bricks left room for the doors and the windows, and it all just happened accidentally. Of course we wouldn't believe that. It amazes me how so many people today believe this of our universe, our earthly bodies, all of creation, all which are far more complicated in design than any building we could ever devise.

Take a look at the moon some clear night and marvel at how it hangs in the sky. When God answered Job out of a mighty storm, He asked:

> Where were you when I laid the earth's foundation? Tell me, if you understand. Who marked off its dimensions? Surely

…Death is the destiny of every man; the living should take this to heart.
Ecclesiastes 7:2 (NIV)

you know! Who stretched a measuring line across it? On what were its footings set, or who laid its cornerstones while the morning stars sang together and all the angels shouted for joy? Who shut up the sea behind doors when it burst forth from the womb, when I made the clouds its garment and wrapped it in thick darkness, when I fixed limits for it and set its doors and bars in place, when I said, "This far you may come and no farther; this is where your proud waves halt?"

Job 38:4-11 (NIV)

I don't think any of us have ever given "orders to the morning, or shown the dawn its place" (Job 38:12, NIV). That makes our daily lists of things to do seem a little trivial, doesn't it? There is so much more to life than today. There is eternal meaning to our being. Many people walking this earth are missing that. They are so focused on this life and what society dictates as important that they miss the eternal element—the all-important element to life and to death.

…Death is the destiny of every man; the living should take this to heart.
Ecclesiastes 7.2 (NIV)

If we do not think on the eternal, we will certainly be caught up in the worldly—the here and now. But if we take enough time to look heavenward and contemplate and get to know this God who created us and the universe where we dwell, we will come to have a much wiser perspective on where we have been, what we are passing over, and where we are going.

We should never take our eyes or our thoughts off Jesus. We need to fix them securely on His face and, like an old song states, "the things of life will grow strangely dim in the light of His glory and grace."

We look up—both spiritually and physically—so infrequently that we oftentimes miss seeing His greatness, His power, His majesty, His holiness, and His undying love for us. If we contemplate on God and the eternal, it will change the course of our lives. We need to start thinking of the heavenly realm, of our great future, of where we will be spending eternity. It will change our priorities here on earth. It will change our life. It will change our death.

...Death is the destiny of every man; the living should take this to heart.
Ecclesiastes 7:2 (NIV)

Let us look heavenward and stop thinking that what we do rotates the earth and makes the world go round. It is God who moves us and the universe.

I'm excited to know God cares for me and lavishes me with a beautiful universe that declares His being and that I will get to meet the true Genius behind our universe, the One who makes our world go 'round, and the Creator of life face-to-face just on the other side of death.

Summary
"Under the Casket: Looking Heavenward"

In our life before death, we need to think deeper and more eternally about our walk here on earth and to understand more our relationship with our incredible God, who lavishes us with a beautiful creation that assures us of His power and love and His presence. It will change how we view both life and death.

…Death is the destiny of every man; the living should take this to heart.
Ecclesiastes 7.2 (NIV)

43

Questions

How can we think about God more?

_____

_____

_____

_____

How can we teach our children to think about God more?

_____

_____

_____

_____

_____

_____

...Death is the destiny of every man; the living should take this to heart.
Ecclesiastes 7:2 (NIV)

How can we "think" more "eternally"?

_____

_____

_____

_____

_____

_____

What does a night sky, a mountain, an ocean say to you?

_____

_____

_____

_____

_____

_____

…Death is the destiny of every man; the living should take this to heart.
Ecclesiastes 7.2 (NIV)

A Dead End:
The Road You're Taking?

> Enter through the narrow gate. For wide is
> the gate and broad is the road that leads to
> destruction, and many enter through it. But
> small is the gate and narrow the road that
> leads to life, and only a few find it.
>
> Matthew 7:13-14 (NIV)

My father-in-law, Wayne, was a wonderful funeral
director. Most families who dealt with him, my
mother-in-law, and Mark were exceptionally
pleased and thankful to have had someone take
such special care of them during their time of grief.
Wayne would agonize over the details of each
funeral. He wanted everything to be as perfect as

…Death is the destiny of every man; the living should take this to heart.
Eccleslastes 7:2 (NIV)

47

he could possibly make it, and he wanted to take away as much pain as he possibly could. During his earlier years, he had a burial that was to take place in a graveyard that he was not too familiar with. He knew there were two roads side by side leading from the highway that looked like they both reached the graveyard that sat far back off the road. However, one led into the cemetery, and the other was a dead end.

He made a special trip to that cemetery the evening before the funeral to make certain of the right road. The next day came, and for some unknown reason, possibly his extreme nervousness at wanting to make certain that everything was just right, Wayne accidentally led the funeral procession down that dead-end road! It was a terrible embarrassment for him. He had to get out of the funeral coach and turn everyone around before he could lead them down the right road.

Can you imagine leading a funeral procession down a *dead-end* road? That must have hit home with a few people in attendance. And besides the unintended pun, it was the road Wayne was trying

…Death is the destiny of every man; the living should take this to heart.
Ecclesiastes 7:2 (NIV)

to avoid. How could he have ended up down the wrong road?

In reflection, I can't help but think about the roads we are offered in life. Sometimes they appear to reach the same destination, but do they really? Certainly, whatever road we take eventually leads to the graveyard. The psalmist states that "Man is like a breath; his days are like a fleeting shadow" (Psalm 144:4, NIV). But what happens after that? The Bible teaches that there are two roads in life. One leads to eternal death and the other to eternal life. We need to contemplate which road we are on. We need to be certain beyond a shadow of a doubt that we know where the road we've chosen leads. We must not become confused because the right road is narrow and many are happily on the wrong one.

In our very short walk on earth, the importance of life is many different things to many different people. There are many priorities in life. Many people strive to gain success in the business world. For many, the purpose of life lies in obtaining as much education as they can. For others, it may be climbing the social ladder. For most, it's more money and power and material goods.

…Death is the destiny of every man; the living should take this to heart.
Ecclesiastes 7:2 (NIV)

And yet we are instructed by Solomon, a man who was granted success and given every pleasure life offers, that none of the above are important.

> I thought in my heart, "Come now, I will test you with pleasure to find out what is good." But that also proved to be meaningless... I denied myself nothing my eyes desired; I refused my heart no pleasure. My heart took delight in all my work, and this was the reward for all my labor. Yet when I surveyed all that my hands had done and what I had toiled to achieve, everything was meaningless, a chasing after the wind; nothing was gained under the sun.
>
> Ecclesiastes 2:1-11 (NIV)

Solomon also pointed out in Ecclesiastes 5 that whoever loves money never has money enough—it just won't satisfy. We are born without anything, and we will die without anything. The old saying "You can't take it with you" should have deep meaning in how we live our lives.

Naked we come into the world, and naked we depart (Ecclesiastes 5:15)—what are we filling up

...Death is the destiny of every man; the living should take this to heart.
Ecclesiastes 7:2 (NIV)

the "in between" with, and will it really matter? I want my life to matter. I want to be on the road that leads to eternal life. I want to be storing up treasures in heaven and not on earth (Matthew 6:19-21).

Solomon, in his wisdom, said, "…Here is the conclusion of the matter: Fear God and keep His commandments, for this is the whole duty of man" (Ecclesiastes 12:13, NIV). It is not our duty to arise each day and put ourselves and our earthly accomplishments as the number-one goals.

Jesus said, "…Seek first His kingdom and His righteousness, and all these things will be given to you as well" (Matthew 6:33, NIV). When we arise each day and ask God to guide our day, to use us, to work through us, to advance His kingdom through us, then we know that we are on the right road, heading in the right direction.

"There is a way that seems right to a man, but in the end it leads to death" (Proverbs 14:12, NIV). Choose carefully!

Is your life being led to enhance God's kingdom, or are you seeking another kind of crown? Are you leading your life to please God, or are you leading your life for the praise of men? What's

…Death is the destiny of every man; the living should take this to heart.

Ecclesiastes 7:2 (NIV)

51

important to you? And more importantly, what will be important when you reach the end of the road you've chosen? What will be important when you come face-to-face with God?

The Lord told Jeremiah to "stand at the crossroads and look; ask for the ancient paths, ask where the good way is, and walk in it, and you will find rest for your souls…" (Jeremiah 6:16, NIV). Are you finding rest for your soul? Or are you tense and desperately trying to climb the ladder (or taking the road that seems right) that belongs to this life and really leads nowhere and ends in death?

One thing I know: We are on paths in this life—they all lead to physical death. We are all on paths to a graveyard. But many of these paths also lead to eternal death. Only one leads to eternal life. Let us right now this very minute stand at the crossroads, look for and ask for the ancient paths, ask where the good way is, and walk in it, and find rest for our souls. God will lead us on the right road if we ask and seek Him. And we too, like the psalmist, can say, "You have made known to me the path of life; you fill me with joy in your presence, with *eternal* pleasures at your right hand" (Psalm 16:11, NIV).

…Death is the destiny of every man; the living should take this to heart.
Ecclesiastes 7:2 (NIV)

Summary
"A Dead End: The Road You're Taking?"

All roads or paths on this earth lead to the graveyard—physical death. We need to contemplate where the road we are on leads. Our lives need to reflect an eternal destination mind-set, and we need to choose the narrow, lightly followed road to eternity.

Questions

What path are you on in life? Why?

_____

_____

_____

_____

_____

_____

...Death is the destiny of every man; the living should take this to heart.
Ecclesiastes 7:2 (NIV)

Where are you going with your relationship with God?

_____

_____

_____

_____

_____

Does your relationship—or non-relationship—with God affect the decisions you make daily? Should it? Why or why not?

_____

_____

_____

_____

_____

_____

...Death is the destiny of every man; the living should take this to heart.
Ecclesiastes 7:2 (NIV)

Spiritually, where would you like to be in five years?
Ten years?

_____

_____

_____

_____

_____

…Death is the destiny of every man; the living should take this to heart.
Ecclesiastes 7:2 (NIV)

A Grave Marker:
My Life, Your Life,
His Life

In the way of righteousness there is life;
along that path is immortality

Proverbs 12:28 (NIV)

Mark and I were to be married soon. His parents
owned the house next to the funeral home in the
small city where he had grown up. We were preparing that house to be our first home. It was only
a hop, skip, and a jump, literally, away from the
funeral home. That meant the house was between
two much-traveled highways and visible—even
the backyard—to all traveling those streets.

...Death is the destiny of every man; the living should take this to heart.
Ecclesiastes 7:2 (NIV)

57

We were remodeling kitchen cabinets, paint-ing, and cleaning. It was exciting to be working there and planning for our future, furnishing our new home-to-be. One possession of Mark's that wouldn't come with us to our new home was Mark's dog, Sam. Sam was an unusual dog—totally mutt, but a mutt that was used to the finer things in life. He lived with Mark and his parents—even had his own bedroom after Mark's brothers and sister were no longer living at home.

Sam could easily discern between New York strip steak and a good prime rib from the doggy bags the family would bring home—he loved prime rib. He could also gobble a sandwich, let-ting the bread roll out of both sides of his mouth but not dropping even a morsel of meat, making certain that it went on to his stomach. I'm sure that you get the picture. He was spoiled. He was dearly loved. And I feared Mark was going to pick him to be the ring bearer at our wedding! Actually, there was talk about that.

As it happened, Sam, at age thirteen, died a few months before Mark and I said our vows. Believe it or not, he did not have a formal funeral! It was surprising to me. However, Mark did decide that Sam should be buried in what was to be our backyard near the house. It was only when Mark was out behind the house digging that grave that I had second thoughts about it. He even used one of the funeral home's grave markers over the freshly dug earth where, below, Sam's carcass was put to its final resting place.

When I saw the scene, I questioned Mark: "Do you know what people are going to think? Doesn't it bother you that people may wonder why a funeral director is digging a grave next the funeral home and putting up a grave marker? I mean, aren't they going to wonder *who* and not *what* is in that grave?"

Mark laughed, but the doggy grave remained. Actually, what would people think? The story made me think more about grave markers and what they say about the person whose physical body lies decaying beneath.

What will your grave marker say of you? What will your life say of you? What will people think? What will God think?—the ultimate question. I've often wondered why some people had huge marble monuments over their graves and others only

…Death is the destiny of every man; the living should take this to heart.
Ecclesiastes 7:2 (NIV)

59

small plaques announcing whose physical bodies lie beneath the grass. Is it only because the amount of money that was available for a marker? Just what is the difference in grave markers anyway?

When I was younger, I noticed that some of my relatives, whom I had grown to love and admire before they died, had only a little monument and I wanted to tell everyone, "I knew him. He was a wonderful person. He was a God-fearing man. That tiny plaque really doesn't reflect him or his life."

Of course, it was much later in life that I realized *the lives we live are our true monuments, not the stones that we lie under.* What is my life and death going to say about me? What is your life and death going to say about you? What did Jesus's life and death say about Him?

How long are we going to be remembered? Is our life truly going to be meaningful to someone else other than our families? Is anyone going to be impressed by what we've done? Is anyone going to be impressed by our *monument?* Will they be impressed because of the help to others we've given along the way or the things we have accu-

...Death is the destiny of every man; the living should take this to heart.
Ecclesiastes 7:2 (NIV)

mulated or the power we had? What will we be remembered for?

There are many who think they've accomplished much in this world—almost everything a person could dream of: fine cars, fine homes, all kinds of honors, awards, and recognitions. They've *made it* in life. But what have they really made? Very few people attain extraordinary fame. Most are quickly forgotten along with all their efforts to *make it* in this life. I recall a poem about the sphinx. There is a wonderful point here.

Ozymandias
Percy Bysshe Shelly (1792-1822)

I met a traveler from an antique land
Who said: Two vast and trunkless legs of stone
Stand in the desert ...Near them, on the sand,
Half sunk, a shattered visage lies, whose frown,
And wrinkled lip, and sneer of cold command,
Tell that its sculptor well those passions read
Which yet survive, stamped on these lifeless things,
The hand that mocked them, and the heart that fed:

...Death is the destiny of every man; the living should take this to heart.
Ecclesiastes 7:2 (NIV)

And on the pedestal these words appear:
"My name is Ozymandias, king of kings:
Look on my works, ye Mighty, and despair!"
Nothing beside remains. Round the decay
Of that colossal wreck, boundless and bare
The lone and level sands stretch far away.

What arrogance! Ozymandias, who apparently thought he was the king of kings, now only has a stone in the middle of decay that marks his existence. The only despair one feels is for this man who thought he was a god but is now gone. Solomon says:

> There is no remembrance of men of old, and even those who are yet to come will not be remembered by those who follow. For the wise man, like the fool, will not be long remembered: in days to come both will be forgotten…Like the fool, the wise man too must die.
>
> Ecclesiastes 1:11, 2:16 (NIV)

Ozymandias's monument says that at one time he was a mighty king whom people evidently feared

…Death is the destiny of every man; the living should take this to heart.
Ecclesiastes 7:2 (NIV)

because of his power, possibly his wealth, his lineage—for whatever reason. Where did all those things considered *important* get him? What good are all those things to him now? The psalmist says it all: "As for man, his days are like grass, he flourishes like a flower of the field; the wind blows over it and it is gone, and its place remembers it no more" (Psalms 103:15, NIV).

It is reported that the great evangelist Billy Graham was asked by talk-show host Larry King, "How do you want to be remembered? I mean, you've had great influence on millions of people all over the world. You've hobnobbed with kings and presidents and other very important persons. After your passing, how do you want us to remember you?"

Billy Graham answered, without hesitation, "That I was faithful to what God asked me to do."

The only enduring fame or immortality comes from knowing and serving a God who is great, a God who is all-powerful, and a God who is a true God. It is only in the way of righteousness and righteous living that there will be true enduring fame and in the life that really counts—the eternal

…Death is the destiny of every man; the living should take this to heart.
Ecclesiastes 7:2 (NIV)

63

one. I want God to know who I am, not mankind. I want to be His, not theirs. I want the eternal to be my priority and where I set my goals, not the physical realm that will soon be no more.

And the exciting thing is that as Christians, our King of kings lives. There is an empty grave. There is no physical stone that holds Him down. He has risen! He's not an Ozymandias, who just thought he was really powerful and important. He is the one who put Ozymandias and those like him in leadership positions. And He is the one who allows us our place on earth—our time to make our monuments. I would certainly rather have that mansion He is preparing for His children than some large stone over my grave or a position of power and wealth here on earth.

We are told by Jesus:

> If anyone loves the world, the love of the Father is not in him. For everything in the world—the cravings of sinful man, the lust of his eyes and the boasting of what he has and does—comes not from the Father but

...Death is the destiny of every man; the living should take this to heart.
Ecclesiastes 7:2 (NIV)

from the world. The world and its desires pass away, but the man who does the will of God lives forever.

1 John 2:17 (NIV)

What will our lives say of us? What will our monuments be? Do our lives resemble Jesus's life, Who lived a life pleasing to His Father? (Matthew 3:17) Will we have a grand marble monument or a grand mansion prepared for us by the One who bought us and made our redemption possible? Just what are our priorities in life and in death? Are we truly *living* and *dying* to meet Him?

Summary
"A Grave Marker: Your Life, My Life, His Life"

We need to think about what our lives are going to say about us. Our real monument is not what is put over our grave but the legacies we leave behind. We need to think about how pleasing our life's work will be for us when we come to the end of the physical realm—and especially how pleased God will be with us. We need to think about what really matters while we're here on earth because we won't be long remembered after death and eternity is forever.

...Death is the destiny of every man; the living should take this to heart.
Ecclesiastes 7:2 (NIV)

Questions

What does your life say about you to this point?

_____

_____

_____

_____

_____

What will your death say about you if you were to die right now?

_____

_____

_____

_____

_____

_____

...Death is the destiny of every man; the living should take this to heart.
Ecclesiastes 7:2 (NIV)

How would you like to be remembered?

_____

_____

_____

_____

_____

_____

How long do you think you will be remembered on this earth after you die? Why?

_____

_____

_____

_____

_____

_____

…Death is the destiny of every man; the living should take this to heart.
Ecclesiastes 7:2 (NIV)

THE ROCK:
JESUS, OUR FIRM
FOUNDATION

So this is what the Sovereign Lord says:
"See, I lay a stone in Zion, a tested stone, a
precious cornerstone for a sure foundation;
the one who trusts will never be dismayed."
                                Isaiah 28:16 (NIV)

It was the age of the pet rocks. Almost every
young person had one. They had names, and some
were even trained—or so they were advertised to
be, and you know you can believe anything that
is advertised! There was a young boy who loved
his grandfather dearly in this age of pet rocks. I
guess the grandchild and grandfather spent much

…Death is the destiny of every man; the living should take this to heart.
                                Ecclesiastes 7:2 (NIV)

69

time together. They had a pet rock that the little boy had painted with his grandfather's help. But it wasn't long after that the grandfather met his destiny with death. I guess it was really hard on the little grandson. He made one request. He wanted their pet rock buried with his dear grandfather. Of course, there was no problem with that. At least no one thought there would be. So before visitation, the little boy slipped the rock over the side of the casket to be buried with his grandfather.

However, what no one considered or thought about was the way caskets are made. They don't have spring systems like beds. Therefore, when the rock was slipped over the side of the casket, it made its way all the way to the bottom of the casket. And, of course, the immediate family, Mark, and his dad were the only ones to know that the pet rock lay beneath the body in the casket.

The real problem arose when, after the funeral, the pallbearers were carrying the heavy casket with its load of death—and rock—out of the funeral home. As they went down the few steps from the funeral home to the awaiting funeral coach, the rock, now at the very bottom of the casket, went

…Death is the destiny of every man; the living should take this to heart.
Ecclesiastes 7:2 (NIV)

rolling, very loudly, to the lower end of the casket and hit with a *thud*. Of course, this repeated at the graveside when the pallbearers carried the casket from the funeral coach and again when they set the casket at the graveside, ready to be lowered into the ground. You could see the nervous eyes moving back and forth and could almost hear people thinking, *What on earth is that noise?*

There followed my life and death lesson. There is a lot of scripture about rocks in the Bible. But they are not rolling rocks or unstable. They are stationary, firm foundation-type rocks. Just a few of those scriptures follow that talk about God being a rock and a refuge who will not change but will remain solid:

> I will love thee, O Lord, my strength. The Lord is my rock, and my fortress, and my deliverer, my God, my strength, in whom I will trust.
>
> Psalm 18:1:2 (KJV)

…Death is the destiny of every man; the living should take this to heart.
Ecclesiastes 7:2 (NIV)

71

Marjorie E. Hopkins

May the words of my mouth and the meditation of my heart be pleasing in your sight, O Lord, my Rock and my Redeemer.
Psalm 19:14 (KJV)

Unto thee will I cry, O Lord my rock.
Psalm 28:1 (KJV)

Bow thine ear to me; deliver me speedily: be thou my strong rock, for an house of defense to save me." For thou art my rock and my fortress...
Psalm 31:2-3 (KJV)

He only is my rock and my salvation; he is my defence; I shall not be greatly moved.
Psalm 62:2 (KJV)

Be thou my strong habitation, whereunto I may continually resort; thou has given commandment to save me; for thou art my rock and my fortress.
Psalm 71:3 (KJV)

...Death is the destiny of every man; the living should take this to heart.
Ecclesiastes 7:2 (NIV)

But the Lord is my defence; and my God is
the rock of my refuge.

Psalm 94:22 (KJV)

It is very obvious that the psalmist saw God as an
unmovable, strong, firm, dependable rock. There was
no rolling around and moving here! We can put our
faith and trust and hope in Him—in life and death!
We don't have to be dismayed about anything.

As a matter of fact, Jesus is a living stone—the
same rock that provided water in the desert for the
Israelites provides living water for us today. He is
a rock that provides salvation so that we won't be
staying in any casket, but we will be resurrected as
Jesus was.

> As you come to him, the living Stone—
> rejected by men but chosen by God and
> precious to him—you also, like living stones,
> are being built into a spiritual house to be a
> holy priesthood, offering spiritual sacrifices
> acceptable to God through Jesus Christ.
> For in scripture it says: "See, I lay a stone

…Death is the destiny of every man; the living should take this to heart.
Ecclesiastes 7:2 (NIV)

73

Marjorie E. Hopkins

in Zion, a chosen and precious cornerstone,
and one who trusts in him will never be put
to shame."

1 Peter 2:4 (NIV)

Jesus is the precious cornerstone, the most important part of the building, and we have the opportu-
nity to be a part of that building

Even though God is a living stone, it doesn't
mean that He changes with the times. He will
always remain dependable and the same forever.
We can count on Him, for He never changes
(Malachi 3:6). Perfection needs no change.

Many feel that we can "update" Christianity—that we can change the rules or *move the rock*
because we are a "modern" society. How far we've
come, it seems to many. We can determine what sin
is or is not because times change—after all, this is
the twenty-first century. But God says He does not
change. In fact, scripture says that "All men are like
grass, and all their glory is like the flowers of the
field; the grass withers and the flowers fall but the
word of the Lord stands forever" (1 Peter 1:24, NIV).

...Death is the destiny of every man; the living should take this to heart.
Ecclesiastes 7:2 (NIV)

DYING to meet HIM

I pray that we will be like the wise man who built his house upon the rock (Matthew 7:25), and when the floods came, he withstood. When the floods of our life come, I pray that we will remain rock hard on our convictions, on our stands, that we will remain a sturdy rock in that building of which Jesus is the cornerstone and the sure foundation.

Summary
"The Rock: Jesus, Our Firm Foundation"

In our relationship with God, He never changes. He is our rock, our firm foundation that holds. He will never force Himself on us but will always be there for us. He is longing to be our firm foundation—and eternal stronghold in this life before death—if we have eternal eyesight to see this truth.

...Death is the destiny of every man; the living should take this to heart.
Ecclesiastes 7:2 (NIV)

Questions

Do you feel you are on firm foundation or slippery rocks? Why?

_____

_____

_____

_____

_____

How do you use Jesus as your rock, your firm foundation?

_____

_____

_____

_____

_____

...Death is the destiny of every man; the living should take this to heart.
Ecclesiastes 7:2 (NIV)

God never changes, so do His laws change?

_____

_____

_____

_____

_____

How do you think God feels about our permissive society? (i.e., what are His views on drugs, sex before marriage/extramarital sex? Have they changed since the New Testament was written?)

_____

_____

_____

_____

_____

...Death is the destiny of every man; the living should take this to heart.
Ecclesiastes 7:2 (NIV)

Loneliness or Holiness: "Well, Who You Got?"

For I am convinced that neither death nor life, neither angels nor demons, neither the present nor the future, nor any powers, neither height nor depth, nor anything else in all creation, will be able to separate us from the love of God that is in Christ Jesus our Lord.

Romans 8:38 (NIV)

I hadn't been married to Mark too long before I heard about Frank. He was an older gentleman that, as far as we knew, lived by himself. He was known to be eccentric and a little strange. Frank made it to almost every viewing we had. Frank was always there. He might not know the family of the

…Death is the destiny of every man; the living should take this to heart.
Ecclesiastes 7:2 (NIV)

79

deceased, probably didn't even know the deceased, but he came to visitation anyway. We always had disturbed family members asking, "Who is that man?" Mark would have to explain.

There were many evenings the funeral home had two bodies—two visitations the same night— just different rooms. On one particular night, Mark was the greeter, opening the door for people to enter the funeral home and directing the visitors to the appropriate room. He saw Frank approaching and, being in a rather rare mood, thought, *I'll get him tonight!*

Mark greeted Frank with a "good evening" and then the carefully chosen words, "Who are you here to see tonight, Frank?" He was certain that Frank wouldn't know and might stumble over his words.

However, without batting an eye, Frank quickly said, "Well, who you got?"

He attended both visitations before he left the funeral home that evening. Upon reflection, I figured he must have been a lonely man. He must have been a man who desperately needed companionship. I wished I'd introduced him to the Lord. For He alone is the ultimate companion to have,

…Death is the destiny of every man; the living should take this to heart.
Ecclesiastes 7:2 (NIV)

the one companion you can always count on, the one companion from whom nothing can separate you from—not even death.

> For I am persuaded, that neither death, nor life, nor angels, nor principalities, nor powers, nor things present, nor things to come, nor height, nor depth, nor any other creature, shall be able to separate us from the love of God, which is in Christ Jesus our Lord.
>
> Romans 8:38-39 (NIV)

Personally, I don't know what I would do without the Comforter, my Savior, and my heavenly Father in my life. I know I would be extremely lonely—desperately lonely—and scared—scared about life and about death.

My mother-in-law, shortly after her retirement, passed away with cancer, and within thirty days, my father-in-law's death followed, after he suffered a stroke sometime before. It was only five days after his passing that my father died, too. It was a very difficult time, to say the least.

…Death is the destiny of every man; the living should take this to heart.
Ecclesiastes 7:2 (NIV)

I prayed I would be with my dad when he died. God answered my prayers. I watched as the spirit of life God gives left his physical body. It made the funeral home visitation so much easier because I knew that wasn't my daddy in that casket; I had already seen him leave and go to God. As I realized the parting between us on this earth was completed, I realized what a truly broken heart felt like, for I certainly had one. I can't describe the desperate feeling I get occasionally when it hits me again that my daddy isn't here anymore. Even though I know it is but a short parting between us, I miss my dad. I miss his presence. I miss his fellowship. I miss *him!*

I know that he is with God. I know he is better off. I know I will see him again someday in a much better life. But I *miss* him now.

I was driving alone down a highway one night on the way back to my home, and the thoughts of my dad came rushing to me. I began sobbing as I thought about this man I missed more than I can describe. I told God how I was feeling, how much I missed my dad. I whispered to God, "I just want to see my daddy." Suddenly, my tears stopped, and

…Death is the destiny of every man; the living should take this to heart.
Ecclesiastes 7:2 (NIV)

I drew my breath in quickly as the thought flooded over me like cold water: *That is how I should feel about God*—my heavenly daddy. I should *long* to see Him *face-to-face*. I should be *longing* to be in His presence, not only on this earth, but in His home! My love for Him should be greater than any love I have on this earth. I think at that moment I realized what Jesus meant and perhaps felt a very small part of what He felt when He said to God in the garden of Gethsemane before His awful death, "Abba, Father," or, translated into our language, "Daddy!"

Yes, we should *miss* our heavenly Father. We should be lonely without Him. And not only this, but God must *miss* us. We were created, by Him, to be in fellowship with Him. We were created in His image, and therefore, because we have these emotions, would not our Father have these emotions? And would not He have that longing to be in relationship with every one of us? It brought a new meaning to me to realize *how much He must miss us*—enough to send His Son to die for us so that we can have a restored relationship with Him and be home with Him one day. You know, Adam and Eve walked and talked with God in a relationship that

…Death is the destiny of every man; the living should take this to heart.
Ecclesiastes 7:2 (NIV)

83

mankind has not had since the fall of man. God wants that fellowship restored. And I believe we all desperately long for that restored relationship, whether we realize it or not.

There is a desperate need in people to feel accepted. There is a desperate need in people to feel a sense of belonging. Most people experience loneliness. In that search for a feeling of belonging, we grasp at cliques in school, clubs, fraternities, and sororities. We buy football jerseys with our favorite player's number to connect ourselves to someone. Some youth even turn to gangs. We all long to belong to something or somebody—to be a part of something. Have you ever wondered why? I believe it's because God created us to be in fellowship with Him, to belong to Him, to be accepted by Him. We lost that at the fall of mankind, and we all have that need remaining in us from the garden of Eden.

I am always amazed at how the stores become ready for Christmas earlier and earlier each year. This year, as I strolled down an aisle of Christmas stuff, I thought about how commercialized the season had become and how early the drive to

...Death is the destiny of every man; the living should take this to heart.
Ecclesiastes 7:2 (NIV)

make money from this season comes. Then I realized it is all possible because of that warm belonging feeling we all crave. Christmas, even to most of the secular world, is usually considered a time for joy, happiness, warmth, family, friends, gifts, etc. It is a feeling we all long for; many just don't realize that to be totally accepted by God through His Son is all they need. They get a substitute feeling, a short-lived one, at Christmastime, even though they sometimes don't truly celebrate the reason for the season.

Love, acceptance, and admiration—we are all seeking these things. Mother Theresa once said, "The biggest disease today is not leprosy or tuberculosis, but rather the feeling of being unwanted." Yet we each are so wanted by our Almighty God. We could not be loved any more by anyone. God made it possible for us to be accepted freely through Jesus Christ.

> For as high as the heavens are above the earth, so great is his love for those who fear him; as far as the east is from the west, so far has he removed our transgressions from us.

…Death is the destiny of every man; the living should take this to heart.
Ecclesiastes 7:2 (NIV)

Marjorie E. Hopkins

As a father has compassion on his children,
so the Lord has compassion on those who
fear him; for he knows how we are formed,
he remembers that we are dust... But from
everlasting to everlasting the Lord's love is
with those who fear Him.

Psalm 103:11-17 (NIV)

No one could be more devoted in obtaining a relationship with us than God our Father through His Son, Jesus Christ. Many of us just don't know it. Now I ask you the question that Frank asked Mark: Who you got? If you have the Lord, it makes all the difference in heaven and in earth. And though God does not exempt us from day-to-day circumstances of life—like death—we don't have to be lonely in our walk on this earth. We can have a unique sense of security, a unique sense of belonging, a unique sense of unconditional love and fellowship until we reach that ultimate fellowship with the Father on the other side of our death. We all should be dying to see our heavenly Daddy!

...Death is the destiny of every man; the living should take this to heart.
Ecclesiastes 7:2 (NIV)

Summary

"Loneliness or Holiness: 'Well, Who Ya Got?'"

People should notice there is something different about us, and we may face difficulty because of this, but we will never be lonely if we have the relationship we need to have with our heavenly Father. He is with us constantly, and we should never feel alone in this physical world because we have the eternal God as our Savior and friend.

Questions

Do you ever feel lonely? Why or why not?

_____

_____

_____

_____

_____

...Death is the destiny of every man; the living should take this to heart.
Ecclesiastes 7:2 (NIV)

87

Do you think you can feel lonely even when surrounded by people? Why or why not?

_____

_____

_____

_____

_____

Do you know people who appear lonely? What do you think you can do to help?

_____

_____

_____

_____

_____

...Death is the destiny of every man; the living should take this to heart.
Ecclesiastes 7:2 (NIV)

How can you overcome being lonely?

_____

_____

_____

_____

_____

_____

...Death is the destiny of every man; the living should take this to heart.
Ecclesiastes 7:2 (NIV)

89

ASK THOSE WE'VE SERVED:
TO SERVE OR TO BE SERVED

Therefore I glory in Christ Jesus in my service to God.

Romans 15:17 (NIV)

How do you advertise for a funeral home? That is a delicate issue in the business. Many funeral homes didn't for a long time, feeling it simply inappropriate. However, a funeral home is like any other business. It is there to prosper, as well as to help grieving families, and in this day and age, many funeral home owners feel advertising is a must—but it has to be very subtly and very tastefully done.

I heard of a funeral home that, I am sure, thought they had come up with delicate way to

...Death is the destiny of every man; the living should take this to heart.
Ecclesiastes 7:2 (NIV)

91

advertise their business. They claimed: *Ask Those We've Served*. My first reaction was to laugh.

"Well, how can I? They aren't talking from the grave, as far as I know!" Of course, I knew what they meant: ask the families we have served. I still laugh at the thought of it today.

But in another context, that question is a very valuable question on how we are advertising our lives. If asked in the context of how many people we have individually served as we live out our lives as Christians before we face death, it can certainly take on a whole new and important meaning. In this look at death and its meaning, there is certainly a look at life and its meaning. Somehow the two are linked so intrinsically, inherently, and fundamentally together that the Apostle Paul says, "I die daily" (1 Corinthians 15:31, NIV).

And we have to ask, "Die to what?" and, "Are we too supposed to die daily?" And if so, "What are we suppose to die from in our daily life? And if we die daily, how can that bring *life?* Are we in service to others? Or are we self-serving? How many individuals have we served throughout our lives, and are we known as servants or self-serving? Just

...Death is the destiny of every man; the living should take this to heart.
Ecclesiastes 7:2 (NIV)

where is our service in this life before death?" I frequently ask myself these questions.

Of course, we find the answers in scripture. We are to die daily to self and take on the activities of a servant. How contrary that is to our world today! We are urged daily by commercials, books, and other forms of communication to *"look out for number one"* and *"take care of yourself,"* because if you don't, nobody else will. *"You deserve it. You have worked hard and earned it,"* and even, *"You're worth it!"* And yet every one of these statements is contrary to what Jesus taught for the purpose of our lives. All those phrases actually mirror words from Satan before his fall from heaven. Listen to his words.

> ...I will ascend to heaven; I will raise my throne above the stars of God; I will sit enthroned on the mount of assembly, on the utmost heights of the sacred mountain. I will ascend above the tops of the clouds; I will make myself like the Most High.
>
> Isaiah 14:13 (NIV)

...Death is the destiny of every man; the living should take this to heart.
Ecclesiastes 7:2 (NIV)

93

It was *I, I, I* all the way—that pronoun appears five times in one verse. But our example, our Jesus, humbled Himself even more than God, becoming a man, when He washed the feet of His disciples and said,

> "Do you understand what I have done for you?" he asked them. "You call me 'Teacher' and 'Lord,' and rightly so, for that is what I am. Now that I, your Lord and Teacher, have washed your feet, you also should wash one another's feet. I have set you an example that you should do as I have done for you. I tell you the truth, no servant is greater than his master, nor is the messenger greater than the one who sent him. Now that you know these things, you will be blessed if you do them."

> John 13:12 (NIV)

I want to be blessed by God. I want to do as Jesus instructs me. It's hard when the fallen human desire for self interferes with our desire to do what is pleasing to God. It's hard to die to self and be selfless. Yet Jesus's total life on earth was as a ser-

...Death is the destiny of every man; the living should take this to heart.
Ecclesiastes 7:2 (NIV)

vant. In just two examples, one at the first of His ministry and one at the end of his ministry on earth, Jesus exudes servanthood. Even at the age of twelve, Jesus knew that He must "be about" His "Father's business" (Luke 2:49, KJV). And as He faced His final entry into Jerusalem, knowing of that terrible betrayal and death that was just hours away, we find Him with His mind "steadfastly" set toward the city when a blind man, Bartemeaus, catches His attention from the side of the street. And what do we find Jesus, the King of kings, saying? "What do you want me to do for you?" (Mark 10:51, NIV).

Jeremiah states that "I know, O Lord, that a man's life is not his own, it is not for a man to direct his steps" (Jeremiah 10:23, NIV). We are here for His purpose—not ours! *We are to die daily to self, to our natural, carnal nature, so that we might live triumphantly as Jesus lived and die triumphantly as Jesus died so that we might live eternally triumphantly as Jesus lives.*

Standing upright, try to picture Jesus on the cross right behind you and aligned with you. When He comes off the cross and becomes alive

…Death is the destiny of every man; the living should take this to heart.
Ecclesiastes 7:2 (NIV)

95

in you, you will have a relationship with the Father. Picture this as a vertical relationship—your head, mouth, and feet would be aligned heavenward with God vertically, and because of this, it ensures that your thoughts will be of God, your heart will belong to God, and your feet will take you where God wants you to go.

Now imagine stretching your arms out, just as Christ's arms would have been stretched out on the cross behind you. I want you to notice that your heart, aligned vertically with God, is also aligned horizontally. Your perfectly aligned vertical relationship with the Father will result in this stretching of your hands outward, and notice that your hands are stretched away from self and opened toward others, allowing God to work through you to reach others.

Serving is the keyword in this life that leads to death. Jesus's life on earth was one of service. He is the King of kings and Lord of lords, yet while He walked on this earth, He was a servant.

Who, being in the very nature God, did not consider equality with God something to be

…Death is the destiny of every man; the living should take this to heart.
Ecclesiastes 7:2 (NIV)

grasped, but made himself nothing, taking the very nature of a servant, being made in human likeness. And being found in appearance as a man, He humbled himself and became obedient to death—even death on a cross! Therefore God exalted him to the highest place and gave Him the name that is above every name, that at the name of Jesus every knee should bow, in heaven and on earth and under the earth, and every tongue confess that Jesus Christ is Lord to the glory of God the Father.

Philippians 2:5-11 (NIV)

While on earth, Jesus was not rich or in search of riches. He was not arrogant or in search of the glory of men. He did not act like royalty as He could have. He served. Why should we think we deserve to be served when the Son of God, the Creator Almighty of all there is, took on the role of a servant? But on the other side of death is where His true exalted identity is known. As so will our identity be truly known after our physical death.

When I face death, I want to face it triumphantly. I want to hear Jesus say, "Well done, good and faith-

...Death is the destiny of every man; the living should take this to heart.
Ecclesiastes 7:2 (NIV)

97

ful servant; you were faithful over a few things, I will make you ruler over many things. Enter into the joy of your Lord" (Matthew 25:21, NIV).

Summary
"Ask Those We've Served: To Serve or to Be Served"

Contrary to what our society teaches, our lives are not for us to please ourselves or to look out for number one but to serve others as the Lord served in His life before His death. We are to work to bring others into relationship with Jesus, teaching them to have an *eternal* perspective on life.

Questions

Are you seeking to serve or to be served? Why?

_____

_____

_____

_____

...Death is the destiny of every man; the living should take this to heart.
Ecclesiastes 7:2 (NIV)

If you are seeking to be served, why do you think others should serve you and how should they serve you?

_____

_____

_____

_____

_____

How can you serve others?

_____

_____

_____

_____

_____

_____

...Death is the destiny of every man; the living should take this to heart.
Ecclesiastes 7:2 (NIV)

How can you serve God?

_____

_____

_____

_____

_____

_____

_____

_____

_____

_____

…Death is the destiny of every man; the living should take this to heart.
Ecclesiastes 7:2 (NIV)

A Sealed Casket: No Turning Back

And it is appointed unto men once to die,
but after this the judgment.

Hebrews 9:27 (NIV)

It was a church funeral—even more formal than ones conducted at the funeral home. On top of that, it was a very fancy, formal church. The funeral service was coming to the end, and the final stage was for Mark and Wayne to close and seal the casket—the final conclusion to the funeral service and to the life of the man in the casket. It is a very symbolic moment. It is the final closure for the fam-

,..Death is the destiny of every man; the living should take this to heart.
Ecclesiastes 7:2 (NIV)

101

ily. It means the end. The finale. The completion. Never to be seen again.

The casket is sealed by turning an Allen-head wrench at the end of the casket that tightens and seals the lid to the casket's base. Wayne had closed the casket, and Mark had completed the sealing task in the front of the sanctuary and in front of all those in attendance. It was only as Wayne turned to walk away that he noticed the front tail of his suit jacket had been accidentally sealed in the casket.

"Open it up! Open it up!" he whispered out of the side of his mouth to Mark at the end of the casket. "I've got my coattail stuck in it."

What an embarrassing moment that must have been! As casually as he could, Mark *unsealed* the casket. Wayne slipped the bottom of his suit coat out, and Mark *resealed* the casket, hoping that no one had noticed.

They probably hadn't. They were probably too blurry eyed to notice anything awry in this final ceremony. But it certainly is an incident that, I'm certain, doesn't occur very often in the funeral business—and one that never occurs in real life. That is, once the casket is closed, there is no turn-

…Death is the destiny of every man; the living should take this to heart.
Ecclesiastes 7:2 (NIV)

ing back. There is no opening of the lid and having a second chance at life after seeing what is beyond death. There is no coming back and changing anything we have done or finishing anything we have left undone. It is the final closure for us. The casket isn't going to reopen and let us out to live our life again. Once our casket is sealed, our life is complete, and we then face the judgment.

"...It is appointed unto men once to die, but after this the judgment" (Hebrews 9:27, NIV). No more opportunities. Will we have regrets? Talk about a time when we will see priorities as they should have been! How will they stack up? When the casket is sealed, it won't matter what jobs we've had, what schools we've attended, what degrees we've accumulated, what organizations we've belonged to, how much money we've had, what kind of a car we drive. All of our earthly accomplishments will crumble away as we stand before God. The only thing that will matter is if we are covered in the blood of Jesus and what we've accomplished for Him.

In Luke, there is the story of Lazarus and the rich man. Lazarus was a beggar, desiring to be fed with

...Death is the destiny of every man; the living should take this to heart.
Ecclesiastes 7:2 (NIV)

103

the crumbs from the rich man's table. When they both died, Lazarus was "carried by the angels into Abraham's bosom: the rich man also died and was buried; And in hell he lift up his eyes, being in torment, and seeth Abraham afar off, and Lazarus in his bosom" (Luke 16: 22, KJV). He cried and asked that Abraham have mercy on him and asked for relief. He also asked Abraham that Lazarus be sent back to warn his father and five brothers "lest they also come into this place of torment" (Luke 16:28, KJV). Abraham told him that "between us and you there is a great gulf fixed: so that they which would pass from hence to you cannot; neither can they pass to us, that would come from thence" (Luke 16:26, KJV).

I've heard people say, "Well, my husband isn't saved. I don't want to go to heaven without him." How could anyone believe that there is any comfort or pleasure or friendship in hell? There will be none—only the "weeping and gnashing of teeth" in a "fiery furnace" (Matthew 13:42, KJV).

I've also heard it said that as long as you believe, you will be saved. But the Bible says, "Thou believest that there is one God; Thou doest well: the devils also believe, and tremble" (James 2:19, KJV).

104

...Death is the destiny of every man; the living should take this to heart.
Ecclesiastes 7:2 (NIV)

There's something much deeper than believing. It's living a life that is completely covered in the Lamb's blood. It's living a life on earth that is in total reliance on Jesus and in preparation for eternity. It is about a relationship that begins in this life and continues through the next.

"Not everyone who says to me, 'Lord, Lord,' will enter the kingdom of heaven, but only he who does the will of my Father who is in heaven. Then I will tell them plainly, 'I never knew you. Away from me…'" (Matthew 7:21-23, NIV). I want God to know me, and I want to know Him! How about you?

It will be a shock to many to realize after physical death there is no turning back. Things can't be done or undone. Relationships can't be changed. Once the casket is sealed, it's not going to be reopened on this earth. As Jesus said at His death "It is finished!" (John 19:30, NIV), it will be finished for us too. He had accomplished His purpose here on earth. Have we accomplished ours?

You know, at death, it is possible to stand before God, and He will see us covered with Jesus's blood, if we have claimed His grace and made Him our Lord and Savior of our lives. He won't see all the

…Death is the destiny of every man; the living should take this to heart.
Ecclesiastes 7:2 (NIV)

105

things left undone, all the things done wrong. He won't see all of our transgressions and all of our sins. He will see the cleansing, beautiful, holy blood of Jesus. He won't see us for what we are; we will not be separated from Him in eternal death because of sin, as we deserve. But we will be held close and dear because of the sanctifying, purifying blood of Jesus. Our judgment is not to be feared! Our casket closing does not have to be a solemn, sad, occasion, but it can be a happy moment when our life on earth is complete and our life, face-to-face with God, is to begin.

Summary
"A Sealed Casket: No Turning Back"

Once we die physically, there is no turning back to re-do or finish what we have left behind. It will be a time when we can see how our priorities of this life stack up to what are really important. Just as Jesus said on the cross before He died—so it will be about our life at physical death—"It is finished." Having eternal perspectives in place during our lifetime will ensure we fulfill our God-given purpose on this earth before we pass into eternity.

…Death is the destiny of every man; the living should take this to heart.
Ecclesiastes 7:2 (NIV)

Questions

Are there things you have left unfinished thus far?

_____

_____

_____

_____

_____

What are your priorities in life? Write them down and reflect.

_____

_____

_____

_____

_____

_____

…Death is the destiny of every man; the living should take this to heart.
Ecclesiastes 7:2 (NIV)

If you knew you were to die tomorrow, what would your priorities be today? Write them down and compare them with your priorities you wrote down for the above question.

_____

_____

_____

_____

How often in a day's time do you "die"? Do you find it easy to die to self? Why or why not?

_____

_____

_____

_____

_____

...Death is the destiny of every man; the living should take this to heart.
Ecclesiastes 7:2 (NIV)

"HEEEEEEEERE'S JOHNNY!": WHERE ARE YOU GOING WHEN YOU CROAK?

> And I'll say to myself, "You have plenty of good things laid up for many years. Take life easy; eat, drink and be merry."
>
> Luke 12:19 (NIV)

I considered myself a pretty good people person. It wasn't always that way, but I felt I had become pretty proficient in introducing myself to strangers by this point in my life, fairly good at talking with them and making them comfortable in the presence of someone new to them. I didn't realize that greeting people arriving at the funeral home and directing them to the casket at visitation would be difficult.

…Death is the destiny of every man; the living should take this to heart.
Ecclesiastes 7:2 (NIV)

109

My first time at greeting visitors at the door quickly made me feel very inadequate to be doing this job that looked so easy. A person entered the funeral home and addressed me with a "good evening" and stated they were here to see Mr. Reynolds. I used my hand and arm in a great sweeping motion toward the front of the room, where the casket stood, and said, "He's right down there." You would have thought I was Ed McMahon saying, "Heeeeeeeere's Johnny!" on the popular late night show or announcing, "Come on down!" to the audience from the game show *The Price Is Right*. I knew immediately, with a sinking sensation, that this wasn't really the appropriate way to direct traffic toward the deceased in the casket. I didn't know whether to laugh or cry.

Looking back, it now it makes me think how the great deceiver, Satan, tries to make a game of life and of death, how he makes us lose track of the focal point of our existence to think lightly of things related to life and death and deeply about the things of the here and now. No wonder God warns us to take death—our destiny—to heart because Satan works all our lives to try to make

...Death is the destiny of every man; the living should take this to heart.
Ecclesiastes 7:2 (NIV)

us forget. Life is not a late-night talk show, nor is it a game show where "he who has the most toys when he dies wins." Life is spiritual, it is deep, and it leads to eternity. One sure wouldn't realize that fact sitting back and watching people scurry and worry day-to-day about all sorts of things that don't really matter. One would think this life is all that has purpose and meaning.

My daughter came to me the other day and was laughing about a bumper sticker she had just seen. It had a frog on it, and it stated, "Where Are You Going When You Croak?" Not a bad statement to think about when we rise alive each new day because we can be sure Satan will be hard at work trying to make us forget that there is an end to this physical life and realm and that it can be just a heartbeat away.

In Luke, there is the story of the man who thought he had life made. It sounds so much to me like many of today's stories.

> ...A man's life does not consist of the abundance of his possessions. And he told them this parable: "The ground of a certain

...Death is the destiny of every man; the living should take this to heart.
Ecclesiastes 7:2 (NIV)

111

rich man produced a good crop. He thought to himself, 'What shall I do? I have no place to store my crops.' Then he said, 'This is what I'll do. I will tear down my barns and build bigger ones, and there I will store all my grain and my goods. And I'll say to myself, "You have plenty of good things laid up for many years. Take life easy; eat, drink and be merry."' But God said to him, 'You fool! This very night your life will be demanded from you. Then who will get what you have prepared for yourself?' This is how it will be with anyone who stores up things for himself but is not rich toward God.

Luke 12:15-21 (NIV)

Wow. This man had his 401(k) in place. He probably had the equivalent of a nice six-figure income. He had a beautiful home and car and a well-manicured lawn. He partied and thought he had it made! How had he come to neglect his soul? Why hadn't he thought about death? Didn't he realize it could come at any moment? Our next heartbeat is never assured. Life was a game to him, and he thought he was the winner. Satan works that way. He's an

…Death is the destiny of every man; the living should take this to heart.
Ecclesiastes 7:2 (NIV)

expert at deception and diversion. He diverts us from where our eyes should be fixed and encourages us to party, to make money, to spend money, to keep busy doing everything that relates to this life and not eternity—to eat, drink, and be merry.

First Peter 5:8-9 tells us to watch out for the work of Satan.

> Be self-controlled and alert. Your enemy the devil prowls around like a roaring lion looking for someone to devour. Resist him, standing firm in the faith.
>
> 1 Peter 5:8-9 (NIV)

If we look at the two major temptation stories in the Bible—Adam and Eve in the garden of Eden (Genesis 3) and Jesus' temptation in the desert after His baptism (Luke 4)—we can see the three major ways Satan worked then and today. In both cases he uses: 1) our appetites—things we want for ourselves; 2) our desire for power, and; 3) he lies, telling us there is no consequence to sin.

Appetite. He tempted Eve with eating of the fruit of the tree of knowledge, both good and evil.

…Death is the destiny of every man; the living should take this to heart.
Ecclesiastes 7:2 (NIV)

113

He tempted Jesus by asking why He didn't turn a stone into bread after Jesus had been fasting forty days and nights and was hungry. Our appetites for food and other physical things for ourselves are very great indeed.

Power. Satan tempted Adam and Eve with power by telling them they would become "like God" if they ate. He tempted Jesus by offering all the kingdoms of the world that God had given him power over.

The third way, lying, seems to be especially rampant today. He tempts by claiming there are no consequences to sin or disobeying God. He told Adam and Eve, "You won't die," like God had told them they would (enter physical and eternal death). Satan told Jesus to cast himself off a high cliff so the angels could rescue Him. True, He would not be hurt, and He could have power over all the world. But it would not be a lasting power but fleeting. God's plan would not be made complete, and the recognition Jesus would gain would not last nor accomplish His purpose for becoming man.

…Death is the destiny of every man; the living should take this to heart.
Ecclesiastes 7:2 (NIV)

Adam and Eve succumbed to temptation—thus here we are. Jesus stood strong and firm—thus we have hope eternal.

We can be sure that Satan is calling our name to "come on down," but it certainly isn't to a game show or for entertainment. Some think hell is a playground of wine, women, and dance. To the contrary, Scripture tells us that hell is: a lake of fire (Revelation 20:15); a horrible tempest (Psalm 11:6); a place of sorrows (Psalm 18:5); a place of weeping (Matthew 8:12); a place of torment (Luke 16:23); a place of no rest (Revelation 14:11); a place of everlasting punishment (Matthew 25:46); a place where they gnaw their tongues (Revelation 16:10); a place of darkness and blackness forever (Jude 13); a place where they beg for a drop of water to quench their thirst (Luke 16:24); a place where they will be tormented with fire (Luke 16:24); and a place where they don't want their loved ones to come (Luke 16:28).

As unbelievably incredible as heaven will be, hell will be as unbelievably a place of torment and torture. We mustn't let Satan make this life a game. There is too much at risk. On the day we lie in the casket, let us be sure that our spirit is with the Lord

…Death is the destiny of every man; the living should take this to heart.
Ecclesiastes 7:2 (NIV)

115

and we will hear him say, "Well done, good and faithful servant; you were faithful over a few things, I will make you ruler over many things. Enter into the joy of your Lord" (Matthew 25:21, NIV).

Summary
"'Heeeeeeeere's Johnny!':
Where Are You Going When You Croak?"

Life is not a game or like a late-night television show for our entertainment. Satan keeps us misdirected and so busy with the here and now that we don't think about death and the eternal. We need to realize the seriousness and importance of what we do while on earth during our very short lifespan because eternity is just a breath away.

...Death is the destiny of every man; the living should take this to heart.
Ecclesiastes 7:2 (NIV)

Questions

If your soul were demanded of you today, would you be ready?

_____

_____

_____

_____

Have you ever felt you have things ready for the future financially? Why could this change over-night? List several reasons.

_____

_____

_____

_____

_____

…Death is the destiny of every man; the living should take this to heart.
Ecclesiastes 7:2 (NIV)

117

How do you think Satan tempts you? By power? By appetite? Or by convincing you there is no consequence to sin? What are other ways you can think of?

_____

_____

_____

_____

What do you think hell looks like?

_____

_____

_____

_____

…Death is the destiny of every man; the living should take this to heart.
Ecclesiastes 7:2 (NIV)

From Death to Life: "Hey, Do You Guys Mind If I Smoke?"

> For in Adam all die, so in Christ all will be
> made alive.
>
> 1 Corinthians 15:22 (NIV)

There was a story that was told among funeral directors. This is one of my favorites. I can't claim that it is true, but it was told to me as the truth. Many times funeral homes have employees solely for the purpose of picking up dead bodies in the middle of the night or, say, during a funeral that is being attended to by the funeral director when he isn't able to leave. These employees don't have to have an embalming license or a funeral direc-

…Death is the destiny of every man; the living should take this to heart.
Ecclesiastes 7:2 (NIV)

119

tor's license; they just need a driver's license and a tolerance of death. Well, it happened that two such guys were sent out to retrieve a body in the wee hours of a cold, wet morning.

A funeral coach, like the one they were driving, is divided back and front with a glass window that can be opened but is usually closed with a curtain over it. These two guys had picked up the body at the hospital morgue and were heading back on a rather long journey to the funeral home, where the body would be immediately embalmed. The young man driving needed to make a restroom stop, and so pulling over at the next available gas station, he headed inside. In the meantime, a hitchhiker came along and knocked on the passenger-side window. The second funeral home employee rolled the window down.

"Hey, man. Can you give me lift?" The rain-soaked hitchhiker asked.

The funeral home employee laughed. "If you don't mind riding back there with a dead body that we've just picked up, I don't mind you riding with us for a few miles."

...Death is the destiny of every man; the living should take this to heart.
Ecclesiastes 7:2 (NIV)

So the hitchhiker entered the back of the funeral coach and settled down near the curtained window beside the covered body. A few minutes later, the driver came back, hopped behind the wheel, and handed his buddy a soft drink, and they continued on their way back to the funeral home. The driver's buddy didn't even think to mention the hitchhiker. It was not long before the hitchhiker had dried out a little and craved some nicotine. But before lighting up, he thought he should ask to see if it was okay. So pulling the curtain aside from the dividing window, he tapped on it and yelled, "Hey, do you guys mind if I smoke back here?"

Now to the second employee, it was not a strange request, but to the driver, who wasn't even aware of the man's presence in the back of the funeral coach, it must have been quite a shock! I mean, it's eerie enough transporting a dead body—but one who wants to smoke? I imagine the driver had trouble keeping the funeral coach on the road. I know it would have been a difficult thing for me to do.

What a great illustration of life after death! "Listen, I tell you a mystery: We will not all sleep, but we will be changed… For the perishable must

…Death is the destiny of every man; the living should take this to heart.
Ecclesiastes 7:2 (NIV)

121

clothe itself with the imperishable, and the mortal with immortality" (1 Corinthians 15:51, 53, NIV).

Yes, we all have to die because of Adam, but we don't face a dark, painful eternity if we have Jesus as our Savior! Because He lives, we too will live! "For since death came through a man, the resurrection of the dead comes also through a man. For as in Adam all die, so in Christ all will be made alive" (1 Corinthians 15:21-22, NIV). From the moment we are born, we are not only facing physical death, but we are facing either eternal life or eternal death. If Jesus is Lord of our life, this beautiful, wonderful thing called eternal life can begin now. "Now it is God who makes both us and you stand firm in Christ. He anointed us, set His seal of ownership on us, and put His Spirit in our hearts as a deposit, guaranteeing what is to come" (2 Corinthians 1: 21-22, NIV).

We can have a taste of eternal life now. It's like receiving a gift and shaking it and wondering what's inside. Yet we only have a portion of it now, for "Now we see but a poor reflection as in a mirror; then we shall see face to face. Now I know in part; then I shall know fully, even as I am fully

...Death is the destiny of every man; the living should take this to heart.
Ecclesiastes 7:2 (NIV)

known" (1 Corinthians 13:12, NIV). The best is yet to come! And that's after our physical death.

Just imagine you have won a major sweep-stakes—your prize is a new 7,500 square-foot home. Wouldn't you be anxious to see it? To claim it? Wouldn't it be on your mind until you're actually there inside that new home?

Jesus tells us that "In my Father's house are many mansions; if it were not so, I would have told you. I go to prepare a place for you…" (John 14:2-3, NIV). It's not just some 7,500 square-foot home—it's a heavenly mansion prepared for us by Jesus!

Shouldn't we be excited to see our mansion that He is preparing for us? If we keep all this in mind, death will not be a dreaded thing for us. For those who truly know the Father and rely on His Son's blood, we can be excited about life after death—for just as physical death passed over the Israelites who had their doors painted with the blood of the sacrificial lamb (Exodus 12:6), if we are covered with the blood of the perfect sacrifice, Jesus, the Lamb of God, eternal death shall pass over us! The grave will not hold us. We can face life after death confidently because God made it so!

…Death is the destiny of every man; the living should take this to heart.
Ecclesiastes 7:2 (NIV)

It has always amazed me how the Bible blends together after being written by forty authors over 1,600 years. It has to be more than coincidence—it has to be because of the divine intervention of God among those He chose to write His holy Word. One example of this is that the Bible ends similar to where it began. In Revelation, John states:

> And he shewed me a pure river of water of life, clear as crystal, proceeding out of the throne of God and of the Lamb. In the midst of the street of it, and on either side of the river, was there the tree of life, which bare twelve manner of fruits, and yielded her fruit every month; and the leaves of the tree were for the healing of the nations. And there shall be no more curse; but the throne of the God and of the Lamb shall be in it; and his servants shall serve him. And they shall see his face; and his name shall be in their foreheads. And there shall be no night there; and they need no candle, neither light of the sun; for the Lord God giveth them light; and they shall reign for ever and ever.
>
> Revelation 22:1-5 (KJV)

...Death is the destiny of every man; the living should take this to heart.
Ecclesiastes 7:2 (NIV)

The tree of life will be back within our reach. (If you remember, access to it was taken away from Adam and Eve after they gave in to the temptation of sin and disobeyed God, Exodus 3:22-24). And our face-to-face relationship with our Father will be restored. We will once again walk and talk with Him. There will be no darkness, no sadness, no evil. It will truly be paradise—not a thing to dread, but rather something to look forward to. Life after death can be for all of us a glorious, beautiful eternal *life*. Praise God!

Summary
"From Death to Life: 'Hey, Do You Mind if I Smoke?'"

Physical death is only the beginning of the beginning. We will be transformed. We will be changed if we belong to God and have Jesus as our Savior. We won't face eternal death and pain but eternal life and joy.

…Death is the destiny of every man; the living should take this to heart.
Ecclesiastes 7:2 (NIV)

125

Questions

Why is our physical death not *the end?*

_____

_____

_____

_____

Are you ready for what we commonly call *the end?* Are you certain of the *beginning of the beginning?* If not, how can you be?

_____

_____

_____

_____

...Death is the destiny of every man; the living should take this to heart.
Ecclesiastes 7:2 (NIV)

Why should we not cringe from death?

_____

_____

_____

_____

_____

_____

...Death is the destiny of every man; the living should take this to heart.
Ecclesiastes 7:2 (NIV)

Are You Dying to Meet Him?: "I'm Going Home"

I eagerly expect and hope that I will in no way be ashamed, but will have sufficient courage so that now as always Christ will be exalted in my body, whether by life or by death. For to me to live is Christ and to die is gain.

Philippians 1:20 (NIV)

Are you ready to die for your beliefs? Are you ready to die for Him if necessary? Are you ready to return the favor that Jesus did for you? I ask myself those questions a lot. Just how deep is my religion, my beliefs, my faith? How firm is the foundation on

…Death is the destiny of every man; the living should take this to heart.
Ecclesiastes 7:2 (NIV)

129

which I stand? How direct is the road I'm traveling on. How eternal are my thoughts? Are my priorities right? Am I anxious to see Him? Am I serving to see Him? Am I living to see Him? Am I dying to see Him?

After several years of being married, Mark decided the funeral business wasn't for him. He accepted another job. The job was a dream come true, so he thought. It was something we had prayed for. It was a very difficult job to attain, but God made it happen very easily for us. And because of this answered prayer, Mark accepted Christ as his Lord and Savior. However, sometimes we beg for things that are not for our best interest. I believe this was one of those times. It wasn't long before Mark hated that job. I know God had answered our prayers, but I believe that it probably wasn't the route He would have taken us had we not interfered by praying for it so fervently. I have heard that in those cases God grants us His permissive will versus His perfect will. But God can always work things out for good to those who love Him and are called according to His purpose (Romans 8:28). I believe that is what happened in this case.

…Death is the destiny of every man; the living should take this to heart.
Ecclesiastes 7:2 (NIV)

However, it wasn't long before Mark began seeking ways to escape this job, which had become like a prison to him. He was so unhappy. His hobby of fireworks was taking a great deal of time and effort. Fireworks—who would ever consider this a full-time job? It was something that Mark was passionate about though, and through our prayers, our fireworks company was born and grew—with the blessings and help of God.

I can't help but think how ironic it is that we went from the funeral business to fireworks. I always tell people that Mark wanted a livelier job! But you know, there's another life and death lesson even here. After death there can be something beautiful for us—much more beautiful than where we came from. Just like after the sad, dreary funeral business, there were these beautiful creations of dazzling light in the sky for Mark and myself.

"Listen, I tell you a mystery: We will not all sleep, but we will be changed. For the perishable must clothe itself with the imperishable, and the mortal with immortality" (1 Corinthians 15:51, NIV). What an interesting and exciting transition that will be—and one that we should dwell on. Why

…Death is the destiny of every man; the living should take this to heart.
Ecclesiastes 7:2 (NIV)

131

should we fear death or not want to think about it when we are told that our wonderful God has prepared things so good for us that we can't even imagine them?

We have lived in a country that has, to this point, been accepting of Christians and religious freedom. More and more though, we hear of persecutions in America—who would ever have believed it—a nation founded on belief in God and on Christian principles? In more and more countries, the Bible is being taught in the schoolroom and in churches for the first time, as America seems bent on closing its doors to the gospel. Today in America, being "tolerant" seems to apply to every religion and every belief but Christianity. It is the beginning of persecution.

Are we prepared to die for our beliefs? We might be called upon to do just that. It is not such an unreasonable question. Many missionaries daily face that question—and even our youth have been called upon to face death for their belief in God (the Columbine High School shootings, for instance). Were not most of Jesus's twelve disciples persecuted unto death? Have not Christians

...Death is the destiny of every man; the living should take this to heart.
Ecclesiastes 7:2 (NIV)

been persecuted through the ages? "Remember the words I spoke to you: 'No servant is greater than his master. If they persecuted me, they will persecute you also'" (John 15:20, NIV). Jesus says it's going to happen. In 2 Timothy 3:12 (NIV), we are told that "...Everyone who wants to live a godly life in Christ Jesus will be persecuted."

We need to be prepared. We need to expect this. Peter tells us, "...Do not be surprised at the painful trial you are suffering, as though something strange were happening to you. But rejoice that you participate in the suffering of Christ, so that you may be overjoyed when his glory is revealed" (1 Peter 4:12, NIV).

We need to be strong. If we have trouble bowing our heads in public to pray because of what people might think, how are we going to stand up and be loyal to Christ if we are asked to die for Him? We are so comfortable in our warm, nicely decorated church buildings. Christianity has become so easy for us. But it's not an easy life to stand for Christ Jesus. The world hated Him—the world will hate us.

...Death is the destiny of every man; the living should take this to heart.
Ecclesiastes 7:2 (NIV)

"If the world hates you, keep in mind that it hated me first. If you belonged to the world, it would love you as its own. As it is, you do not belong to the world, but I have chosen you out of the world. That is why the world hates you" (John 15:18, NIV). If you love the world, if you feel comfortable here, beware. This is not our true home—that is to come on the other side of death and our lives here better be in preparation for our true home—the one that will stand throughout eternity.

When my sister, Nancy, sees or hears things that are worldly, evil, totally opposite from godliness, she will shake her head and say, "This world is not my home." You know, the only way we can stand up and admit our beliefs and our allegiance to our God without fear of death is if this world is not our home. *You can't let go of things that are dear to you unless you have something dearer to hold onto.* The only way we can stand up for our beliefs is if we truly know the one who made us believe. The only way we can stand up for our beliefs, even unto death, is to have our eyes fixed on the eternal and on the one true God. The only way we can die for our beliefs is to understand that death is truly our destiny, and there

...Death is the destiny of every man; the living should take this to heart.
Ecclesiastes 7:2 (NIV)

is nothing on earth to compare with what God has planned for us if we have accepted Him. "…'No eye has seen, no ear has heard, no mind has conceived what God has prepared for those who love him'" (1 Corinthians 2:9, NIV).

Paul said, "I am ready not only to be bound, but also to die in Jesus for the name of the Lord" (Acts 21:13, NIV). He tells us, "For I reckon that the sufferings of this present time are not worthy to be compared with the glory which shall be revealed in us" (Romans 8:18, KJV).

I pray that we can truly say, like Paul,

> "Whether I live or die, it doesn't matter. If I live, I get to serve Jesus and if I die, well that's even better yet because I'll be with the Lord" (Philippians 1:20).

I want to be like that. It is my prayer that you do too. This world is not my home. I'm only passing through, and though I'm only a mist, a vapor that appears for a short time, what I say and do here matters more than anything else in my life because it determines my eternal destination—my true home. The only way I, or you, can stand up for our Christian beliefs is if we are truly *dying to meet Him.*

Summary
"Are You Dying to Meet Him?: This World Is Not My Home"

If we know God and love Him, we, like His first disciples, will live and die for Him. We will have that eager expectation of meeting Him face-to-face. It is an anticipation that we achieve by thinking eternally all the days of our life.

Questions

How strong do you feel your faith is?

_____

_____

_____

_____

...Death is the destiny of every man; the living should take this to heart.
Ecclesiastes 7:2 (NIV)

Have you ever felt homesick for God and godly things, or do you feel perfectly comfortable and content in this world? Why or why not?

_____

_____

_____

_____

_____

Do you think you could physically die for your spiritual beliefs?

_____

_____

_____

_____

_____

_____

...Death is the destiny of every man; the living should take this to heart.
Ecclesiastes 7:2 (NIV)

Marjorie E. Hopkins

Do you have an eager expectation of, or a longing for, meeting Him face-to-face?

_____

_____

_____

_____

_____

_____

_____

_____

_____

_____

_____

...Death is the destiny of every man; the living should take this to heart.
Ecclesiastes 7:2 (NIV)

CLOSING PRAYER

Show me, O Lord, my life's end and the number of my days: let me know how fleeting is my life. You have made my days a mere handbreadth; the span of my years is as nothing before you. Each man's life is but a breath. Man is a mere phantom as he goes to and fro: He bustles about, but only in vain. He heaps up wealth, not knowing who will get it. But now, Lord, what do I look for? My hope is in you. (Psalm 39:4-7, NIV)

...Death is the destiny of every man; the living should take this to heart.
Ecclesiastes 7:2 (NIV)